IMAGES
of America

AROUND MALVERN

A mid-1880s scene shows a primitive downtown. The center building was occupied by Newhon and Belding offering dry goods and footwear. Located at 103 North Reed Avenue and burning in 2009, it housed Mason's Grocery for years. Later, Pizza Rack/Pizza Works occupied the location. The next building shown was the W.C. Lewis Tin Shop, which was razed in 1940 to build Red's Nite Club. (Courtesy of the author.)

On the Cover: A proud group of men at the Big Four Clay Company pose for this early 1900s photograph. Joseph A. Reed is shown seated in the mine car nearer the front. Chartered in 1902, this company was near Bethlehem Cemetery. Four men totaled the number of initial promoters who pushed for the creation of this business, which is how the name was chosen. (Courtesy of the author.)

IMAGES
of America

AROUND MALVERN

Jason N. Lombardi

ARCADIA
PUBLISHING

Published by Arcadia Publishing
Charleston, South Carolina

Printed in the United States of America

Library of Congress Control Number: 2024933912

For all general information, please contact Arcadia Publishing:
Telephone 843-853-2070
Fax 843-853-0044
E-mail sales@arcadiapublishing.com

Visit us on the Internet at www.arcadiapublishing.com

*Dedicated to my family, friends, and community who have supported
and encouraged my love of Malvern history since my youth.*

CONTENTS

ACKNOWLEDGMENTS

Reflecting on the more than 30 years of my love affair with Malvern history, it is nearly impossible to publicly thank all those who have guided me. My family has humbly been my greatest stand behind, beyond what words can describe. You are my heroes. I spent immeasurable days with people such as John R. Gwynn, Esther F. Reed, Isabel B. Brothers, and Bertha C. Richards. They unselfishly devoted their time to me as I plunged into our history. As I write, a movie plays in my mind of time spent with these individuals along with countless others. These memories make me one of the richest men alive.

Frances L. Montella, who became a dear friend, and I cofounded the Malvern Historical Society in 1994. I thank the amazing volunteers at the society who continue to ensure history remains alive, preserved, and appreciated. Roger David Hardesty, Douglas P. Angeloni, Craig S. Bara, and Tyler A.P. Moody deserve special thanks. Through the years, while pasting together the pieces of this work, invaluable friendships have been made and continue.

I would be amiss to omit some of my ethereal counterparts who shared a mutual appreciation of local history and took an active role in preservation during their day. William A. "Art" Lewis, in the 1930s, published historical photographs in the *Malvern News* with valuable details. Ralph L. Albrecht, the local historian during the Malvern centennial celebration, went to great lengths to gather and record our story. Thank you to these individuals for their insight into recording for tomorrow.

Sincere thanks to those who have permitted me to scan photographs and glean details from your memories. The list of names is lengthy. Due to space limitations in this book, it is unfeasible to include everything and every family. Please know, if your photograph has not been included here, it still remains a valuable asset to my files. Research is an ongoing endeavor. Unless otherwise noted, photographs in this pictorial history are from the personal collection of the author.

Of course, thank you to Malvern for being the best hometown ever.

INTRODUCTION

It is often the most unassuming places that hold some of the most fascinating history. Lives are lived, and days pass by without much thought into the yesterday of our beginnings as life continues to advance. The village of Malvern, Ohio, has existed as a place to call home for more than two centuries. Settlers arrived and carved into the hillsides a community: a place to call home. People, by nature, long for roots and establishment, a place to exist, return to, and remember. The readers of this pictorial history are carving a place into the story of Malvern, just as our pioneer ancestors did.

Today, little remains of the magnificent empire founded on the roots of the clay industry here. Stepping back roughly one century ago, inhabitants and visitors alike would have witnessed a skyline embellished with smokestacks from any of the multiple clay plants and factories here. This industry put Malvern on the map. Articles in news publications labeled this village of roughly 1,200 citizens "the pioneer clay city" of the United States. Bricks and products bearing the Malvern name were shipped across the country daily to pave streets and create cities. The opportunities seemed endless.

Dream makers and visionaries Moses Porter and Richard Vaughn traveled to this area in 1806, with Porter laying claim to the grounds respectfully known as Malvern today. Porter Street is named in his honor. Vaughn settled closer to present-day Oneida. By felling trees and clearing land, this area began to seemingly evolve from a blank canvas. Word spread of this new location in the infant state of Ohio, with others following suit.

A pioneer member of the Methodist Church in the states and an impassioned abolitionist, Rev. William Hardesty arrived in this area around 1816 from Columbiana County, Ohio. Here, he constructed a mill powered by Sandy Creek, and from this point, business began to flourish. Hardesty, not unlike Porter and Vaughn, was an enthusiastic visionary and realized promise in this region. Building a substantial brick residence overlooking the area near present-day East Main Street, Hardesty's two-story dwelling remains the oldest known standing structure in Malvern: a testimony to the sacrifice and gratifying determination of one man. Hardesty knew potential and platted the original village of Troy here in November 1834.

Troy was a small locale on the north bank of Sandy Creek and only consisted of five primitive dirt streets. For reasons unknown at the time of this writing, it was decided to change the name of the new settlement of Troy to Malvern on February 26, 1840, just a little over five years after having been platted and named. This change was completed during the lifetime of Hardesty, and one can speculate why the name changed and who made the official decision.

The year 1836 marks when another tiny hamlet sprouted up on the south bank of Sandy Creek and was graced with the title of Lodi. This community was platted by Esquires James Reed and William E. Russell, with the original plat map marking the Sandy and Beaver Canal as having a direct connection to this new village. The platters had high expectations the canal would reach their destination; however, the waterway would ultimately follow the north bank of Sandy Creek in favor of Malvern (formerly and briefly Troy). Lodi did continue to grow but never achieved incorporation nor had its own post office. A large German populace inhabited this village early on. Lodi would remain its own entity for decades and at some point simply faded into history as a place name.

The Sandy and Beaver Canal was being planned into existence as of 1827 and expected to head through this location. The Malvern segment was completed in 1845 and saw some commercial use. The arrival of the railway in 1853–1854 and issues with flooding led to the canal becoming void as a profitable venture.

Expanding through the years, Malvern proper has been the home of several houses of worship and multiple school buildings. The first documented school in this vicinity was built on the west side of Robertsville Avenue about one-half mile from town. This was a log schoolhouse. Sometime around 1840, a school was built at 214 East Porter Street, with this structure still standing as a private residence. As the population increased, these were followed by other buildings. Numerous one-room schoolhouses dotted Brown Township to meet the educational needs of rural children. In 1928, a high school was built on West Main Street, with other additions to this structure through the years providing a place of learning until the current building was constructed in 2016.

From mills, grocers, blacksmiths, shoe shops, jewelers, and tinsmiths to bakeries, a moving picture theater, a chocolate factory, and an outdoor movie theater, businesses continued to lay their tracks through Malvern soil. History has been appreciated in this area over time. Rev. George Hardesty pleaded at the county level for the formation of a historical society in 1858: a man ahead of his time. Hardesty asserted, "The early settlers of our county are fast passing away, and with them, many interesting incidents of early life among us are being consigned to oblivion. A few yet remain who braved the dangers of pioneer life, who would cheerfully lend their aid in carrying out the objects of such a society." Through the pages of this pictorial history, the footsteps and interests of Hardesty are being followed in preservation efforts to record the story of a place.

Collecting and recognizing the history of a community with more than 200 years of happenings is a challenging undertaking. With careful consideration, images for this pictorial history have been selected to explore the story through time as related to Malvern, Ohio. Omissions were unintentional, with some areas of this community's timeline less thoroughly documented in photograph form than others. As details continue to be revealed through collection, research, and study, these additional fibers of the fabric woven together in a tapestry of pride and a sense of belonging will perpetuate this remarkable story.

Returning in near full circle, we revisit the Hardesty name to conclude this introduction. Hiram H. Hardesty, of this village, published an extraordinary historical atlas of Carroll County. His efforts at historical preservation are akin to his brother George, as related to detail and thoroughness. In summation, the author of this pictorial history directs special attention to wording penned in 1874 by Hiram, which appears to speak directly to the author at hand, "It would be useless to disguise from the reflecting man the fact that the citizens of Carroll County have not yet caused their territory to yield to the full capacity of its soil, and its hidden mineral wealth. . . . Hence, we may look forward without misgiving to a future more brighter and more prosperous than even the past has been; and he who shall be called upon to write the succeeding pages of this history may be congratulated in advance upon the rich material for study which is to be placed in his hands."

One

HOME IS WHERE
THE HEART IS

An 1870s stereoscopic view card reveals the Hardesty homestead. It has been said the brick home took three years to construct, finishing in 1827. Overlooking Malvern at 225 East Main Street and built by Rev. William Hardesty, this home was a safe house on the Underground Railroad. Artist Clyde Singer was born here in 1908, and the home remains the oldest known standing structure in Malvern. (Courtesy of John Champer.)

Located at 103 East Main Street, this Italianate structure is one of Malvern's oldest, dating most likely from the 1840s. Built by the Hardesty family, with David Hardesty being an early occupant, Dr. Enoch C. and Cordelia (Paessler) Ross resided here during the latter half of the 19th century. Ross was associated with William McKinley, and McKinley stayed in this home with the Ross family while visiting the area.

This pioneer farm, located at 9156 Leopard Road NW between Oneida and Pekin, has been known as the Snyder farm for decades. Revolutionary War veteran Richard Vaughn traveled to this area in 1806 and was the original proprietor of this property. His remains are buried on-site at the Bever cemetery, with death occurring in 1821. The image here dates to around 1908, and this home is no longer standing.

Dr. Jonathan Moffett and his family are shown outside their home at 100 East Porter Street. This was the birthplace of telephone industry pioneer Theodore Vail in 1845. His father, Dr. Davis Vail, built the home around 1840, operating his practice here. A town pump was located on the side porch. This home was moved in 1903 and still stands at 119 Second Street. Contini Insurance Agency now occupies the site.

The Patrick C. Hull home at 8187 Blade Road NW in Oneida is listed in the National Register of Historic Places. Built in 1837 by Henry Bever, the Greek Revival home has been lovingly restored. The McCall family owned this residence as did local historian Ralph Albrecht. Situated in the middle of Oneida's business district, this structure was near the canal, mill, and railway. This photograph was taken in 1907.

An early residence in downtown Malvern, this home stood at 110 East Porter Street. Next door to the Malvern Historical Society, the building was donated to this organization for restoration. Unfortunately, beyond reasonable repair, the home was razed in 2006. The gazebo currently occupies the site. Many believed the home to be of log construction, but this was found to be inaccurate during demolition. This photograph was taken in 1998.

Ohio senator Albert R. Haines built this fine home opposite of Bethlehem Cemetery and called it Church Hill Farm. At that time, Bethlehem Presbyterian Church was located within the cemetery. It is believed the home pictured was built in the late 1850s or early 1860s. This structure is said to have burned, and the Queen Anne–style home currently on-site at 7326 Canton Road NW took its place.

The Rukenbrod home located at 5116 Citrus Road NW still stands today as a private residence. Pictured standing on the ground are Hammond Rukenbrod, at far left; his son Leas Rukenbrod, standing at near middle; and spouse Jennie (Roudebush) Rukenbrod, at far right. The others are likely some of their other children. Hammond was a son of Dr. Solomon Rukenbrod, who practiced in the Malvern area.

Another early home in Oneida is said to have been built by Henry Bever in approximately 1837. Bever was a grandson of settler Richard Vaughn. Located at 8237 Blade Road NW, this residence has a unique second-floor porch area. Past occupants include Amos E. and Harriet (Adams) Buss as early as the 1850s. The home passed to their daughter Mary Louise, who married Rev. Jasper S. Ross, a Civil War veteran.

The former George Locker home is located at 3250 Tower Road NW. Built in the early 1860s, rumor has it as being a canal lockkeeper's house on the Sandy and Beaver Canal. This has been proven inaccurate as the date of construction was roughly a decade after the demise of the canal system through Malvern. A log house once stood next to this home. (Courtesy of C.W. Baker.)

The former Roy Pearson home on Alliance Road NW, opposite of the former Little Forest Inn, was built in 1851 by Baxter A. Blythe and affectionately called Blythewood. The property passed to his son Robert Thompson Blythe and his wife, Emma (Creighton) Blythe, with their accomplished artist daughter Sarah (Blythe) Beatty being raised here. (Courtesy of the late Robert Kitzmiller.)

Ulysses Grant Thompson, pictured second from the left, proudly poses outside of his Oneida home, which still stands at 8201 Old Canal Lane NW. Thompson was born in 1868 in Oneida and served that community as postmaster and operated the mill. At that time, the area was known as Oneida Mills. This home is likely another early example of Henry Bever's design and construction. (Courtesy of Florence Thompson Untch.)

This grand brick home was once known as the Squire Tidball residence. Razed in the late 1960s or early 1970s, the home sat at 3103 Alliance Road NW and was situated nearer the roadway. A mobile home now occupies the lot. The Tidball name has substantial roots in the area; however, the full history of the owner and this property is limited.

The Creighton mansion (built 1877) was owned early on by A.B. Creighton and later James Ross Creighton and was located at 5077 Alliance Road NW. Following use as a private residence, the property served as the Crawford Nursing Home. Prior to demolition, the Jaycees hosted haunted houses in the empty building. Woods Grocery built its final location here in 1984. Kishman's Fresh Market IGA currently occupies the site.

Nellie (Rukenbrod) Penick, pictured in 1907 at left, writes on the reverse of this postcard photograph that she was "picking grass out of the walk" when someone stopped by to offer to take her picture. This home still stands at 233 East Grant Street. The child is simply labeled as Chalice with no surname provided.

Built possibly in the early 1870s, this home was owned by the Ross family. It appears on the 1874 map of Malvern as published in the *Illustrated Historical Atlas of Carroll County, Ohio* by Hardesty. This structure was built at 231 East Porter Street in the Ross family's addition to Malvern, which indicates it likely belonged to Samuel and Angeline Ross. This family deeded nearby property to the Christian Church in 1873.

Built as the residence of Mayor Charles W. Ruff and his wife, Josephine, 325 West Main Street stands today and still retains some of the original features, including leaded glass windows. The date of construction is unknown; however, it is believed to be within the first five years of the 20th century. Charles was the father of two daughters: Helen, born in 1903, and Esther, born in 1911. (Courtesy of Sonia Strock.)

The late Harwood C. and Ella (Elson) Ross residence is constructed of Malvern-made bricks. Malvern was booming with the clay product industry during the early part of the 20th century, and this home proudly displays some of the community's ware. Ross was part owner of the Malvern Fire Clay Company, which produced hollow building tile and would later be known as Kopp Clay. The address is 802 East Porter Street.

The home at the right stands at 123 South Bridge Street and once belonged to Abby Bortz. The small frame residence at the left has been gone for decades. The old hotel, which still stands, can be seen in the background near the center. The brick structure at the extreme left was the auto garage of Fred W. Noel and was known as Handy Service Repair Company in the late 1920s.

Taken in September 1925, this home still stands at 307 East Porter Street. The reverse of this photograph reads, "James Caldwell with wife and sister." Research reveals Caldwell (the builder of this home) married Luella Reed in 1893. His unmarried sister Jennie resided with him for many years. The Caldwells, before moving to this brick home, resided on a farm on Middle Run Road in the present-day Lake Mohawk area.

John L. Campbell built a brick ranch home behind his former filling station at the southeast corner of North Reed Avenue and Canal Street. Due to the construction of Ohio State Routes 183/43 through Malvern, Campbell had the home moved in 1962 to its current location at 7229 Harding Drive NW. This photograph shows the move while on Canal Street at the intersection of Canton Street. (Courtesy of Michael Campbell.)

Nationally recognized artist Clyde Singer was raised in this home, which once sat at 120 West Water Street behind the current bank. The Singer family shows up in records residing here as early as 1930. The home was burned for practice by the local fire department decades ago. Singer painted many scenes from this dwelling. Other than this connection to art world fame, little is known about the structure's history.

Clyde Singer made a name for himself in the world of art. Born and raised in Malvern, where his father worked at a local brickyard, Singer exhibited his work nationally and was associated with the Butler Institute of American Art for 55 years. Studying in New York, some of Singer's prized works have fetched upwards of $170,000. Singer died in 1999. (Courtesy of the Malvern Historical Society.)

Dr. David L. Everhart resided and practiced medicine in this home, which still stands at 117 South Canton Street. The family of the doctor states the structure was built around 1890. Everhart obtained his degree in 1896 and began practice in Malvern in 1913. In 1920, Everhart is shown residing here with children Ward, Bernice, and Claire. His spouse, Margaret, died in 1918, and Everhart died in 1924. This image was captured around 1915.

The George and Elida Klotz home at 503 West Main Street still stands today. Klotz, former Malvern mayor, farmer, and shoemaker, built several homes in Malvern, including this one in 1891. Seen in this c. 1911 photograph are two of his grandchildren, Forrest Klotz (left) and Bessie Mick (right). The Frank and Catherine Morris family resided in this home built next to the school for many years.

Built by Harry Haskey in 1891, this home (still standing) is situated at 516 North Plain Street. Haskey, a native of England, was Malvern's lamplighter, with his shop advertising incandescent gas lamps seen at the right. Pictured here are, from left to right, possibly granddaughter Helen Ruff, Haskey, and Hattie (Fishel) Haskey. Harry and his wife died on the same day in February 1930. (Courtesy of Sonia Strock.)

James Nelson Robertson built this home once located at 224 East Porter Street around 1899. This photograph was taken in 1906. Along with his wife, Mary Emma, records show their children being Howard, Helen, and Kathryn. Robertson and his brother William Emmet founded a plumbing and hardware business in 1898, which continues on as Robertson's Building Center. This home burned in 2002 with an empty lot remaining.

Known as the Deckman-Bartley Funeral Home and located at 434 West Main Street, this structure was built as a private residence (in 1907) by Lee Dell Scott Klotz. Deckman purchased the property for its current use in the 1930s. Klotz, an 1891 graduate of Malvern High School, was not only a former mayor and school teacher, but also served on the school board and was superintendent of the Whitacre-Greer Fireproofing Company.

In 1953, this home was moved in preparation for a new bank (open house in January 1954) to be built at 123 North Reed Avenue. The home shown here was built on that lot early on and moved to its present location at 319 East Porter Street Rear. Some past residents (when at its original site) include Levi Pariso, the Whittington family, Chalmers and Bertha Davis, and Russell and Agnes Barrick.

Luella Rennier called 323 East Grant Street home as early as 1910. She is shown living here with her parents, George and Adaline, at that time. Rennier was born in 1877 and spent the majority of her adult life at this residence. Teaching piano to local residents, her eccentric ways led to her living a reclusive life, with the teacher of music never marrying. This photograph of the home was taken around 1908. Below is Rennier (proudly seated at center) with some of her piano students and their mothers. From left to right are (first row) Mabel Weaver, Bertha Reed, five unidentified, Mable Stackhouse, and seven unidentified; (second row) three unidentified, Rennier, and two unidentified; (third row, standing) Alice Weaver, two unidentified, Viola Stackhouse (marked with x), sixteen unidentified, Eulalia Weigand, and six unidentified.

John F. and Della (Swisshelm) Fisher called 208 South Reed Avenue home during the first part of the 20th century. Fisher was manager of the Deckman-Duty Brick Company in Malvern and also served on the school board. This home is made of rock-faced Malvern brick. Behind the home is the cupola of the St. Martin Lutheran Church when it was located in that building, now occupied by American Legion Post 375.

James E. Finefrock appears to be the builder of this home located at 400 East Porter Street, likely built in the early 1890s. Finefrock was a school superintendent and sold the property to the Harsh family in 1896. Carrie (Haines) Moses, daughter of Ohio state senator Albert R. Haines, also resided here for several decades. This photograph dates to around 1910. (Courtesy of Stephanie Skinner.)

Henry and Caroline (Richards) Gween can be found living at this home at 222 Bridge Street as early as 1900 with several children. Records list Henry's occupation as a clay miner at one of Malvern's brickyards, with this home being just feet from one of the plants. Pictured here in this c. 1910 photograph are, from left to right, Caroline Gween, John R. Gween (later spelled as Gwynn), and Matilda B. Gween.

Grocer Samuel F. Totten resided in this home located at 209 Bridge Street around the turn of the 20th century. In 1903, he built his storeroom at 111 North Reed Avenue, and during warmer weather, he rarely wore shoes while manning his business. This habit earned him the nickname of the "barefoot salesman." The home still stands and retains much of its original features.

Another example of Malvern-made brick, this home at 122 West Porter Street was occupied by the Yockey family for decades. This photograph dates to around 1910, with Harlan and Della Yockey moving in around 1912. Their son Herbert, who served as Malvern mayor from 1958 to 1962, was born in this home in 1917. The rock-faced style of brick here is also found at the Malvern United Methodist Church.

This early structure possibly dates to the 1830s or 1840s and is located at 122 West Wood Street. This section of present-day Malvern was part of the original settlement of Troy, which was platted in 1834. At the time this photograph was taken in the early 1900s, the Thomas and Caroline Pearson family resided here. Many will recall the Dunn family occupying the home at one time.

The busy state route that passes by this home today was a mere dirt street when this photograph was taken around 1906–1907. Located on the northwest corner of the intersection of Alliance and Blade Roads NW, the home is shown with a buggy parked on Blade Road NW. The Reed family were residents here when this photograph was taken and were most likely the builders. Abraham Boyer Reed was born in this home in 1909.

Once situated across from the thriving Deckman-Duty Brick Company, this brick home still stands at 5072 Citrus Road NW. The Miller family was residing here in the early 1900s when this image was captured. Two daughters, Vayla and Vesta, are shown together in the carriage. Row house-type dwellings were once directly to the right of this structure and likely related to brickyard company housing. (Courtesy of Diane Martin.)

An 1874 map shows this property belonging to William Denny Robertson, with the current address being 6877 Alliance Road NW. Robertson was married to Alice Rogers, and together they had a large family. Two of their sons (James Nelson and William Emmet) established a plumbing and hardware business, which still continues as the Robertson Building Center. This grand brick home with its stone wall still stands.

George Deckman likely built his home on the west side of North Reed Avenue between the bridge and Canal Street. This home was across the alley, which paralleled the former Hollywood Brands building. Deckman is pictured seated in the second row, third from left. He established the Deckman Furniture Factory in 1861. James and Mary Marmo were some of the last occupants here. (Courtesy of the Malvern Historical Society.)

Built as the Laubender home at 229 East Porter Street, this structure still stands, having been constructed in 1890. Widow Mary Barbara Laubender and her daughter Ruth had this residence constructed with materials purchased at the Fishel and Buel lumberyard on West Main Street. The exterior image was taken in 1928. Daughter Ruth would remain in this home alone following her mother's death in 1901 for nearly 50 years. She never married and was described by those who knew her as well-educated, brilliant, and somewhat eccentric. Talented with painting, she mentored nationally recognized artist Clyde Singer during his younger days. Speaking several languages, she attended the Art Institute of Chicago, along with having a pastime of raising butterflies. The interior photograph reveals the home's typical Victorian-era living room with homeowner Mary Barbara pictured. (Below, courtesy of Jimmy Montella.)

Two

FAITH OF OUR FATHERS

Bethlehem Presbyterian Church was organized in 1822 and originally adjoined Bethlehem Cemetery. The first building (constructed in 1824) was replaced with the structure shown here in 1848. The church was near the current Civil War soldiers' monument and faced Alliance Road. Services here ceased in 1893 as congregants built a new church in town. The remainder of the building shown was sold to John Worley, moved, and used as a sheep barn.

Leaving the original location at Bethlehem Cemetery in August 1893, members of Bethlehem Presbyterian Church built this new frame structure the same year at 423 East Porter Street. Many parishioners split from the church when it was decided to abandon the building at the cemetery. The original slate roof of this building had colored slates spelling out the words Bethlehem on the east side and Presbyterian on the opposite.

A rare stereoscopic view of the German Reformed Church dates likely from the 1890s. Occupying the east half of lot 157 on East Grant Street, this building was moved to Malvern from 5400 Hein Avenue SE in 1891. It once stood next to the former Wildwood Chapel, being built there in 1837. Around 1927, Robertson's occupied this building and operated its business here for a number of years.

Liberty Chapel, just outside of Oneida on Paris Avenue SE, has a scant history. No specific denomination can positively be attached to this house of worship, which was within the bounds of Liberty Cemetery. The aging structure had been empty for decades and was razed in July 1996. Most former residents with knowledge of the church recall it being nondenominational, with others stating those of the Baptist faith worshiped here.

St. Martin Lutheran Church is pictured here around 1900 at 233 Bridge Street. This building was constructed in 1871 and served as a house of worship until 1940 when the congregation built a brick church on West Main Street. In the 1940s, Charles Buck managed Buck's Hall here, which held many square dances, wedding receptions, and community gatherings. Valley Post 375 of the American Legion currently occupies this building.

Building a new house of worship is an exciting event for a community. Shown here on April 28, 1940, is the laying of the cornerstone at St. Martin Lutheran Church at 301 West Main Street. From left to right are Leah Dutenhaver, Edward Beach, and Paul Dutenhaver. This time capsule was opened on May 19, 2019, and the final service was held in the building on June 2, 2019.

First Baptist Church of Malvern traces its roots to 1918, beginning as a Sunday school mission. This initial group met at Village Hall until 1923 when the congregants reorganized, appointed a pastor, and began meeting in a small brick building on the grounds of Robinson Clay Products Plant No. 7. The building, shown here in 1959, was constructed in 1928 and was replaced with the current structure in 1989. (Courtesy of the Malvern Historical Society.)

St. Francis Xavier Roman Catholic Church and rectory are visualized in this c. 1910 photograph. The first church building was constructed in 1848, with cemetery burials predating this. The present brick church was constructed in 1884. The rectory was built in 1892 with this congregation being established in the community of Lodi.

Pictured is a c. 1935 interior view of St. Francis Xavier Roman Catholic Church. Kerosene lights provided indoor illumination as late as the early 1910s, and pews were constructed of lumber supplied by the Fishel and Buel lumberyard on West Main Street. Many alterations have been made to this building through the years, with extensive changes made in 2001 and 2002 when the interior was reversed. (Courtesy of Kay Laubacher Bosh.)

Built in 1873 at a cost of around $4,000, this church was known as the Disciple Church, the Church of Christ, and now the First Christian Church. Early on, seating was divided with men assigned to the west side and women to the east. Remodeled in 1911, this building, located at 325 East Porter Street, saw more significant changes in 1992 and 1993 when it was converted into Linwood Apartments.

Fashionable women pose at the Church of Christ, located at 325 East Porter Street, around 1912. Pictured are, from left to right, (first row) five unidentified, Pearl Dolvin, and two unidentified; (second row) Augusta Reed, two unidentified, Nettie Reed, Anna Gorrell, and three unidentified.

The original First Christian Church of Malvern building was sold, heavily remodeled, and converted into the Linwood Apartments. This photograph was taken in January 1993 during that process. As the changes occurred, structural aspects of the inner 1873 core building were revealed. The bell tower was part of the 1911 remodeling. This congregation constructed a new church just east of this building at 4046 Coral Road NW.

Located at the corner of Wood and Canton Streets, this 1842 structure served as the first house of worship for the Methodists. Initially known as the Methodist Episcopal Church, Rev. George and Hannah (Hillerman) Hardesty were leading members and donors. The brick structure shown here was razed in 1896, and the current church building stands on the same corner. Rev. Thomas W. Anderson is pictured here shortly before demolition.

The United Methodist Church has been worshiping in this building since 1896. Built of Malvern-made brick, the edifice was designed by architect Sidney Badgley, with the total cost to finish and furnish it being just over $4,500. William McKinley was present for the laying of the cornerstone. The building contract was with Fishel and Buel, and while this structure was being constructed, services were held in the German Reformed Church on East Grant Street.

Taken in 1949, this photograph shows the second parsonage for the Malvern United Methodist Church, which was purchased in 1879 for $1,000. Facing Wood Street, it was east of the church with a parking lot in its place. Construction on the current ranch-style parsonage began in the fall of 1963, replacing this frame home, which was razed soon thereafter. The first parsonage still stands at 109 East Wood Street.

Three

EDUCATIONAL FOUNDATIONS

West Main Street was bustling with activity when this photograph was taken in 1969. This unique aerial shot shows the new elementary classrooms being constructed around the former 1891 structure. At that time, the 1891 building housed elementary students only but initially held all grades from first through seniors. A new gymnasium is also shown here under construction. Ceasing as school property in 2016, it now houses Damascus Friends Church.

Constructed as a school around 1840, this building still stands as a private residence at 214 East Porter Street. It continued to be a house of learning until sometime in the 1850s. Early teachers here were a Mr. Daniels and a Mr. Nichols, with this school being constructed to alleviate crowded conditions in and walking distance to a log school built on Robertsville Avenue.

As the community grew in size, this small school was erected near the home presently situated at 605 West Wood Street. Known as "the little brick," this building was constructed in 1846 and torn down sometime around 1919. The soft red brick left over from the demolition of this building was used in part of the foundation of the home constructed on this lot by Arthur Leyda, which still stands.

Known by different names including Malvern Select School, the Academy, and Malvern Seminary, this tuition-based school opened in 1859 and was located at 104 Wood Street. Founded by Dr. John H. Tressel, the school's program taught multiple languages along with instrumental music, writing, drawing, and painting. Classes ceased here in February 1892. The building was razed in 1933 or 1934; however, the old stone wall shown in the photograph remains today.

Built in 1891 of Malvern-made brick, this grand schoolhouse served the community until its demolition in 1970. William McKinley was on-site when this building was dedicated at its West Main Street location. A grand stairway led to the second level, with the third floor originally containing an auditorium/gymnasium. The large bell from this school remains as the football field victory bell at Malvern Village Park.

The first graduating class of Malvern High School in 1890 poses for posterity in this rare photograph. From left to right are (first row) Superintendent Prof. James E. Finefrock and Alice E. Pendergast; (second row) John E. Deckman, Henry Vinton Buel, and John A. Maurer.

The entire student body is photographed around 1910 in front of the 1891 schoolhouse on West Main Street. The builder of this structure was Ross Rue, and the stone steps were the scene of countless class photographs through the years. The name and cornerstones are shown to the right of the doorway, with these relics rescued by the Malvern Historical Society and now on display at the Malvern Village Park.

When this 1891 schoolhouse was demolished in 1970, its contents were auctioned off, including the slate chalkboards and wooden school desks. Records indicate there were four classrooms on the first floor of this building and four on the second floor. This structure was rescued from a fire in 1928, with the entire east side gutted by the blaze. The architects of this grand edifice were Kramer and Zoll.

Fire escapes at the 1891 schoolhouse on West Main Street were the scene of class photographs, as seen in this c. 1923 image. Iconic first-grade teacher Laura E. Creighton is pictured here with her students. Creighton taught roughly 50 years and was descended from one of the pioneer families of the area. She died in 1955 and remained unmarried, devoting her adult life to the children of Malvern.

The former Malvern High School was built on West Main Street in 1928. Currently, Damascus Friends Church occupies the building. The cornerstone of this building was laid in June 1928 and was attended by roughly 4,000 people. The first day of classes held in this new building was January 2, 1929, with the cost to build this brick structure being around $80,000. Classes ceased here in 2016.

One-room schoolhouses were scattered throughout the township to meet the educational needs of rural families. Pictured here is the second Oneida school, which was located at 9069 Blade Road NW. Constructed likely in the 1860s, the building had been converted to a private residence years before its demolition. The building was empty and gutted as of January 2010 following a fire. This photograph dates from around 1908.

Taken in approximately 1885, Oneida children are shown in front of their one-room schoolhouse. The teacher (Basil Early) is pictured at the right. Of special note, pictured in the back row at the far right is Irvin T. Brothers, who would later become an area photographer. His photographs have surfaced throughout the years, and many are included in this pictorial history. (Courtesy of the Malvern Historical Society.)

Turkey Hollow schoolhouse still stands as a private residence at 5243 Krone Road NW. This building is believed to have been constructed around 1868, and it has been remodeled. It is unclear when classes ceased at this location, but it appears to be at least 1917 based on other class photographs found taken at this location.

The Stars and Stripes are proudly displayed for this 1898 photograph taken at Turkey Hollow schoolhouse. The teacher, Lee Dell Scott Klotz, is shown at the left alongside his pupils. Klotz typically addressed himself as "Dell" or "L.D.S." Jokingly, when students would inquire what his initials stood for he would reply, "Lord Delaware Stanton." Klotz also taught at Oneida school and a term at Crossroads schoolhouse in 1893–1894.

Brown Frame schoolhouse still stands on the corner of Bellflower and Lilac Roads NW. This building was constructed in 1888 by Fishel and Buel, whose business was located on West Main Street. Early directors of this school include Jacob Grunder, John McCauley, and Levi Miller. Classes ceased at this location in 1941 with a community center taking over the property for local meetings and functions.

Crossroads school, built in 1865, was once located at 3029 Lemon Road NW. Records reveal it was unofficially termed Watson school in honor of a longtime nearby resident, likely Isabella Watson. A road that no longer exists traveled roughly north/south nearly next to this school and intersected present-day Lemon Road. Therefore, the school was named for the intersection of two roadways. This photograph was taken in 1907.

Upper Telpahak school still stands and is currently occupied by a house of worship. Located at 4419 Robertsville Avenue SE, the present brick structure was built in October 1900. It replaced a prior school on this site, which dated to at least 1870. Multiple variations of the name Telpahak have surfaced through research with a nearby roadway still bearing this name.

Lower Telpahak school has been gone for many years and was situated at the intersection of Avalon and Layrd Roads NW on the northeast corner. Pride Valley mobile home park would be just south of where this schoolhouse once stood. It was still being used as of 1910 but vanished from records after this.

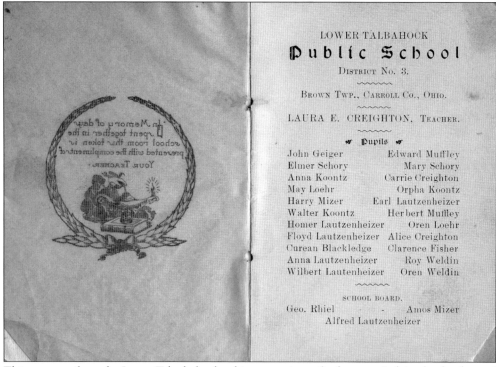

LOWER TALBAHOCK

Public School

DISTRICT No. 3.

Brown Twp., Carroll Co., Ohio.

LAURA E. CREIGHTON, Teacher.

Pupils

John Geiger	Edward Muffley
Elmer Schory	Mary Schory
Anna Koontz	Carrie Creighton
May Loehr	Orpha Koontz
Harry Mizer	Earl Lautzenheizer
Walter Koontz	Herbert Muffley
Homer Lautzenheizer	Oren Loehr
Floyd Lautzenheizer	Alice Creighton
Curean Blackledge	Clarence Fisher
Anna Lautzenheizer	Roy Weldin
Wilbert Lautenheizer	Oren Weldin

SCHOOL BOARD.

Geo. Rhiel - Amos Mizer
Alfred Lautzenheizer

This program from the Lower Telpahak school is a rare piece of ephemera. Judging by the dates of birth of some of the pupils listed through research, it is believed this dates to the early 1900s. The teacher is listed as Laura E. Creighton, with several other familiar surnames, including Koontz and Geiger. Note the peculiar spelling of the school name. (Courtesy of Kathy Bortz.)

Chestnut Ridge school was once situated on Lander Road NW. This school was unofficially known as Lewis Ridge due to nearby residents bearing this surname. The Chestnut Ridge neighborhood was a generalized area near the school, flanked by Avalon Road NW on one side and Bellflower Road NW on the other. Limited information is available, but the school existed in 1874 and was still in use as of approximately 1915.

A c. 1890 photograph taken outside of Chestnut Ridge schoolhouse provides only one person's identity out of the entire group. Pictured in the fourth row, sixth from the left, is Bert Lewis. Other early surnames, in addition to Lewis, who were in the vicinity of this school would have been Bortz, Buck, Ebner, Laubacher, Leyda, and Stoltz.

Dublin school has a scant history. The photograph here dates to 1910 and is a rare image. Originally built between 1865 and 1870, the school was on the Robertson farm and moved twice to new locations on that same property. The building was located in the 8000 block of Lardon Road NW between Largo and Lark Roads NW. It was razed in 1930.

Sandy Valley Items.

The Minerva postoffice was broken open last Friday night. The burglars failed to get into the safe, hence they did not get much.

Decoration at Malvern was largely attended. Mr. Karns, of Canton, delivered the address. The Dell Roy band furnished the music, which was highly appreciated.

J. R. Neely has gone to Ada to attend school.

Jos. Bell is employed to teach the Middle Run school next winter.

Miss Anna Brandon closed her term of school, at Turkey Hollow, last Saturday. She commenced at Morges on Monday.

Jacob Weaver, Sr., has purchased a fine top buggy. About the next article he gets, will be a new wife.

The Literary Society of Malvern will give an entertainment the evening of June 10th.

May 3, 1881.   DALTON.

Middle Run school is referenced in articles such as this, which appeared in the June 2, 1881, issue of the *Carroll Republican*, alerting readers Joseph Bell would be teaching. Other instructors included Robert Blythe and Pearl Gamber. In 1874, the schoolhouse was shown in the southeast quarter of section 30 in Brown Township (current Lake Mohawk area). A small nearby waterway, called Middle Run, is how the school was named.

The Malvern football team poses in an area on Water Street in this November 1909 photograph. Pictured are, from left to right, (first row) George Logan and Paul Wilson; (second row) Charles Logan, Norville Moore, Ben Burwell, Walter Weigand, and Fred Deckman; (third row) Cullen Yost, Clyde Willis, Harry Kriger (sp?), and William Burwell.

In 1931, the Malvern High School girls' basketball team was Carroll County champions. Shown next to the high school on West Main Street are, from left to right, coach Mark Weaver, Anna Robertson, Dorothy Williams, Dorothy Hiner, Margaret Ellen Reed, Lucille Laubacher, Gretchen Reed, Winona Duell, and Kathleen Darby. Coincidentally, the boys' team also claimed the county championship that same year.

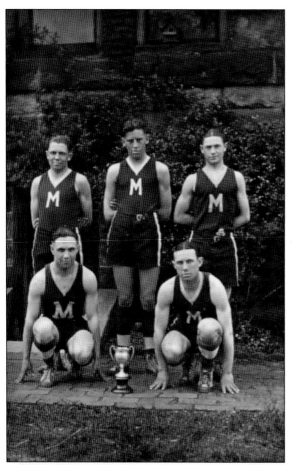

The Malvern High School 1922–1923 school year undefeated basketball champions pose with their trophy outside of the school on West Main Street. Pictured are, from left to right, (kneeling) Howard Baxter and Ray Logan; (standing) Forrest Klotz, Bob Spratt, and Myron Eckley. Uniforms were the responsibility of the players and typically handmade, so variations will be seen. Note the birdhouse on the window behind the players.

This charming photograph was taken around 1913 and shows some fellow Malvern High School classmates cooling off in the water. Pictured are, from left to right, Augusta Hermann, Bessie Mick, Cora Scheidecker, Lena Rhiel, Mary Hermann, Viva Dumbleton, Margie Laubender, and Louise Keffler. The majority of those pictured graduated high school this same year.

Four

PIONEER CLAY CITY

This 1887 photograph captures the first brickyard crew in Malvern. Pictured are, from left to right, (first row) Henry Gween, William Reed, John Kratz, O.A. Roudebush, Christ Murray, Amandus Keffler, and Ross Rue; (second row) Gilbert Richards, Henry Hoffman, George Davis, William Caldwell, Frank Hoover, David Fetters, and William Fetters; (third row) Thomas Moore, Henry Totten, Wilford Summers, James Sautters, George Neidlinger, Ed C. Gaily, William Gascon, and David Richards.

Pictured is a glimpse at the Big Four Clay Company in the early 1900s, where working in the mines was a dangerous and exhausting occupation. Paving bricks were first manufactured at this plant in 1903, with one million bricks produced per month. During World War I, this company made material for government contracts and was awarded for the superior grade of their wares by the US War Department.

Seen here is another early brickyard scene, likely from the 1890s, when child labor laws were virtually nonexistent. Several young boys, some even barefooted, are shown with the workforce. Often the younger crew was responsible for providing water to the employees and fitted with a bucket yoke. Several dippers would be included with the buckets for the men to drink from. (Courtesy of the Malvern Historical Society.)

The first clay plant in Malvern was located on the south side of town; it was later known as Robinson Clay Products Plant No. 7. In the spring of 1886, John Kratz explored the area in search of hidden clay deposits. An abundance was discovered, and Kratz took into partnership Ross Rue. This first official plant was built during the winter of 1886–1887. The image here dates to around 1900.

Having experienced the ravages of time, this 1890s photograph is a superb example of a typical workforce at a local brickyard, including a dog. Three are identified in the first row; starting fifth from the left, they are Harwood Ross, James Davy, and Lee Dell Scott Klotz. Ross later managed another local clay plant, Davy later owned a grocery, and Klotz became mayor.

The clay industry became the life force of Malvern early on, as seen in this early-1900s photograph at a Deckman-Duty Brick Company mine. Around the turn of the 20th century, the railway system was in full force, with clay products being shipped out daily to areas across the United States.

This early-1900s photograph of the plant that would become Robinson Clay Products Plant No. 7 demonstrates how rapidly the industry was growing. Most knew this business simply as No. 7. From humble beginnings, the firm of Kratz and Rue developed into a thriving industry. The first kiln of fire-clay brick in the Sandy Valley was burned at this site with a crew of six men and three boys.

Little evidence remains of the once-grand empire pictured here around 1910. The last smoke stack was toppled in 2016, which forever changed Malvern's skyline. Business leaders from all parts made this village a stop. Attention from the brickyard industry aided in building up other businesses in town such as restaurants and boarding. The population of Malvern in 1900 was around 700 and growing.

The sheer magnitude of ware stacked and ready for shipment is unbelievable in this c. 1920 photograph. Robinson Clay Products purchased this plant in 1901 with the company transitioning from manufacturing paving brick to sewer pipe, as seen here. The tower of Bethlehem Presbyterian Church on East Porter Street is in the distance.

Taken around 1928, this photograph shows a few employees of Robinson Clay Products Plant No. 7 enjoying a quick break for a snapshot. Pictured are, from left to right, Emerson Hewitt, Lawrence Patton, Carl Crissinger, Charles Buck, John Reed, Jerome Kocher, Reverend Holt, Elijah Jenkins (seated), Walter Harsh, Ralph Williams, and two unidentified.

Former company housing near the brickyard for employees of Robinson Clay Products Plant No. 7 is shown here in a state of abandonment. The whistle at this brickyard blew at 5:00 a.m., alerting workers when to show up for work, and again at 6:00 a.m. It sounded throughout the day at 11:30 a.m., 12:30 p.m., and 4:30 p.m. and became an institution of its own.

Organized in 1887 as the Malvern Clay Company, this brickyard was located on Morges Road; a mobile home park now occupies the site. For the superiority of the product, this plant's entry won a gold medal at the 1893 world's fair and once again in 1904. Bricks found in and around Malvern have an image of the awarded gold medal stamped into the surface, which makes them quite recognizable.

This rare image shows the main engine room at the Deckman-Duty Brick Company. The Malvern Clay Company was sold to this firm in 1908. John Fisher was plant manager here at one time, and locals unofficially termed this brickyard as "Fisher's Works." Transitioning to the manufacture of hollow building tile in 1927, nothing structurally remains to mark the company's existence.

Malvern-made bricks were used to pave village streets beginning in 1915, which is shown in this photograph. The firm of Ward and Patrick was hired to oversee the completion of the job with a price tag of $35,000. One of the first streets in town to be paved was West Main Street. Local residents completed the majority of the work, with no brick streets remaining in the village.

Formerly located at 3266 Coral Road NW, this plant was the last to operate in Malvern. Most recently known as Kopp Clay, this brickyard was incorporated on October 26, 1911, as the Malvern Fire Clay Company. Construction began in 1912, with the plant burning in 1919 and being rebuilt the same year. This brickyard also offered company housing to employees.

The Malvern Fire Clay Company was unofficially known as "Ross Works" by locals due to Harwood Ross holding the offices of president and manager. In 1921, the daily output from this plant was about 250 tons of burned ware with a workforce of approximately 100 men. This company also received recognition from the US War Department for the superiority of its product during World War I.

While all plants at Malvern utilized the natural resource of clay, not every plant produced brick. The Malvern Fire Clay Company changed names multiple times, including the Malvern Clay Company and the Malvern Flue Lining Company Inc. Hollow building tile was produced here for years. This photograph dates from the 1920s and was taken at this plant.

The Big Four Clay Company was built behind and to the east of Bethlehem Cemetery. The original four promoters of this corporation included John Kratz, who discovered clay in Malvern; G.O. French; Dr. W.A. White; and Monroe Kratz. This company also produced hollow building tile. This image dates to around 1910.

The Pittsburgh and Malvern Clay Company, organized in 1904, was located on the back way to Waynesburg (Citrus Road). Hollow building tile was also produced here. Pictured are, from left to right, (first row) Frank Smith and Jerome Kocher; (second row) two unidentified, Jasper Johnson, Adam Burwell, and Jakie Kocher; (third row) three unidentified and Howard Burwell. The company closed in 1930. (Courtesy of the Malvern Historical Society.)

Many families emigrated from Europe to Malvern just to seek employment at one of the local brickyards. This photograph was taken approximately 1912 and shows a diverse group of workers, predominantly Italian, at the Whitacre Fireproofing Company (formerly the Pittsburgh and Malvern Clay Company). This brickyard also offered company housing for employees.

The Whitacre Fireproofing Company would later be known as the Whitacre-Greer Fireproofing Company. This c. 1910 photograph likely captures some office staff at the plant. Supt. Lee Dell Scott Klotz is pictured in the window at left. Klotz served many roles within the community and is credited as being a strong proponent for the advancement of Malvern.

A group of men pose with a piece of early equipment at one of the local brickyards, with miners being easily identifiable by the carbide lamps on their hats. Many would spend the majority of their day underground pulling clay for manufacture. Frank Reed (second from the left) is the only person identified in this photograph taken around 1910.

The end of an era is represented in this photograph captured Easter Sunday 1976 when fire destroyed the former Robinson Clay Products Plant No. 7 on the south side of town. This business was permanently closed in 1957 following another fire at that time. Studying this image makes it difficult to fathom a thriving industry here producing 15 million bricks annually. (Courtesy of Kay Laubacher Bosh.)

Five

THE EXCHANGE OF GOODS

This rare scene provides a look at the milling industry here roughly in the 1870s. The mill at right is lettered with "Malvern Mills," "cash for wheat," and the owners' names, "Davis and Baxter." These mills were situated at the present-day intersection of North Reed Avenue and Canal Street. The mill at right burned at some point, while the mill at left remained until 1959 (minus the cupola).

Taken in the early 1900s, this image shows a pioneer business block at 109 East Main Street. This tired train of buildings once housed Malvern's first mayor's office and a post office. Records indicate it was built around 1846, with Rev. George Hardesty serving as first mayor in 1869 after village incorporation. It is believed this photograph was taken as a record of existence prior to the demolition of the structures.

Situated on the southwest corner of the intersection of North Reed Avenue and Canal Street was the Lewton House, a popular boarding facility. Proprietors Abraham and Susan Lewton, along with their family, opened the business venture in 1876 at this location. The Lewton House later moved to 216 South Reed Avenue, with this second building still standing as a private residence. (Courtesy of the Malvern Historical Society.)

James Harsh purchased this building in Oneida in March 1891 and opened a general store for the community. The post office was also located in this structure, which was situated nearly across from the restored Greek Revival home at 8187 Blade Road NW. The Harsh family has deep roots within Carroll County history.

An early building once located at 407–409 North Reed Avenue, this structure saw many businesses through the decades. The center door gained entry to William Burwell's home for years, while the door on the left was the way to step into Rollie Thompson's barbershop. Charles G. Deuble had a jewelry and silverware business in the early 1890s, also on the left-hand side.

Malvern Village Hall has been located at 116 West Main Street since 1915. The structure is an early one made of soft red brick. From approximately 1866 until around 1883, Theophilus H. Paessler operated a general store here. Around the turn of the 20th century, the Malvern Garment Factory was in business here, with some recalling the seamstresses making clothing items to send overseas to World War I soldiers. (Courtesy of the Malvern Historical Society.)

The Malvern Garment Factory employees are shown on the steps of the present Malvern Village Hall at 116 West Main Street. These were the days of old treadle sewing machines; the Malvern Historical Society is privileged to own one from this business. Some people are identified, from left to right, (first row) unidentified, Flora Crawford, three unidentified, Zelma James, Eva Reed, and unidentified. The photograph is from around 1906.

This is another superb portrait of employees of the Malvern Garment Factory. This photograph dates closer to 1900. Note the variety of fabrics displayed in their clothing, which they no doubt made. One person is identified and is pictured in the second row at the far right (Iva Reed Logan). The owner of the company is thought to be either a Mr. Greer or Weir. (Courtesy of the Malvern Historical Society.)

With a fascinating history, this building had its beginnings in Oneida and was moved to its present location at 203 North Reed Avenue in 1900. Thought to have been constructed in the 1870s, this business place hosted a number of restaurants early on but spent the majority of its time here as a hardware store. Many will recall William Wirebaugh as the owner for decades. This photograph dates to approximately 1908.

Before electricity made its way to town, Malvern employed a lamplighter to address the multiple gas lampposts scattered around town. His position required him to light in the evening and extinguish in the morning. Pictured here with his lamp-lighting bicycle is Harry Haskey, who held this role around 1900. Haskey was a native of England and took up residence on Plain Street. (Courtesy of Sonia Strock.)

On the square at 103 South Reed Avenue was the J.K. Davy grocery store, shown in this c. 1914 photograph. Davy operated here from 1908 until 1914. During this time, the upstairs was occupied by shoemaker Adam Maurer. A brick facade was later added to the front and remains. Pictured are, from left to right, unidentified (in shadow), unidentified, Frank Keffler, unidentified, Dorothy Bixler, Chattie Davy, James Davy, and unidentified.

Ross and Son Pharmacy was located at 103 North Reed Avenue, with Civil War veteran Dr. Enoch C. Ross founding the business in 1887. His physician's office was located on the second floor, with that practice beginning in 1870. Son Harwood was a junior partner and is pictured here at the center. Note the elevated bandstand to the left. This building burned in 2009, and an empty lot remains.

Charles Kirkpatrick and his wife, Sadie, operated a grocery store in this building, which still stands on the southwest corner of the intersection of North Reed Avenue and West Main Street. William Dickey and John McCauley operated a grocery here in the 1880s, calling it the Bee Hive Store. Kirkpatrick began his business in 1913, with the building later being purchased by Erma Thompson, where she operated Thompson's Restaurant.

The Malvern Mills was the heartbeat of the village during the second half of the 19th century. Multiple members of the Hardesty family were part of this business. This mill was situated at the current intersection of North Reed Avenue and Canal Street. Demolition was imminent when the state route came through Malvern, and the mill fell to the wrecking ball in 1959. This photograph dates to around 1910.

A popular place to ice skate and swim was the forebay next to the Malvern Mills. This area assisted the water to the wheel to initially power the mill. Malvern's water wagon, which was used to keep the dusty streets at bay, would fill up at this location. In this 1911 photograph, one can see the old Hardesty homestead on East Main Street in this distance.

When this photograph was taken around 1905, Thomas Tewel operated a general store in a building he constructed in 1891. The Knights of Pythias and other organizations held meetings upstairs. The state liquor store occupied the first floor for many years, with the Malvern library being in the small section to the right. The parking lot for the current post office at 116 East Porter Street occupies the site now.

Dr. William R. Spratt and his wife, Nancy, resided at 117 West Main Street. Directly to the west of his home was this small doctor's office, where he practiced for decades. The space remains vacant to this day. Spratt, who is pictured at left, finished medical schooling in 1865. Note the ancient structure at the left, which occupied the neighboring corner lot. (Courtesy of Kelly Nypaver.)

Harsh's Lunch was opened on November 3, 1947, at 623 West Main Street by Charles and Mable Harsh, who resided one door to the west. This eatery was popular with students due to its proximity to the school. The business was out of operation by around 1964. The home has been remodeled and remains a private residence. (Courtesy of Doug Schmidt.)

This 1902 photograph reveals the crew from the Deckman Furniture Factory, which once sat on the west side of village hall. Pictured are, from left to right, (first row) Harry Burwell, Roy Reed, Frank Burwell, and Sam Reynolds; (second row) Joseph Swisshelm, Harry Deckman, William Shaw, Conrad Deckman, and G. Herman Klotz; (third row) Lee Dell Scott Klotz and Stephen G. Deckman, both managers. (Courtesy of the Malvern Historical Society.)

H.E. Myers Restaurant and Confectionery was operating at 203 North Reed Avenue when this photograph was captured around 1925. Proprietor Myers is standing in the center of the doorway with Mary Hahn at right. Mary's sister Bertha Hahn operated a restaurant in this same building from 1919 to 1922. The building has changed hands many times through the years and remains a local landmark by the bridge.

An empty lot now occupies the site where Edward I. Poole operated a poolroom. Located at 111 South Reed Avenue, Poole purchased this building around 1907–1908 and resided on the second floor with his family. He was a nationally known early baseball player and lived out his remaining years in Malvern, dying in this building in 1920. The property later passed to his daughter Mary.

Baseball great Edward I. Poole is shown here with some Malvern friends in this c. 1916 photograph. Poole spent the majority of his life in Malvern and raised his family here. Pictured are, from left to right, (first row) Richard Poole (mascot); (second row) two unidentified, Poole, and Fred Deckman; (third row) three unidentified, Stephen Deckman, and unidentified. (Courtesy of the late Richard Miller.)

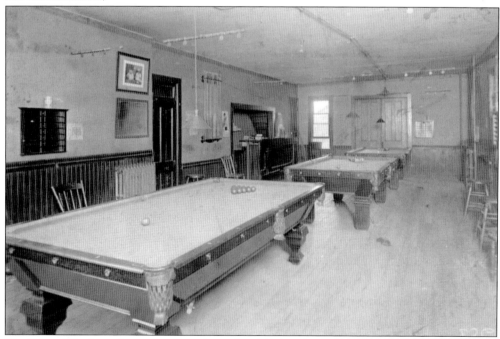

The Edward Poole poolroom was once located at 111 South Reed Avenue. Poole resided upstairs of his business. Ryan's Variety Store (1940s) occupied the spot, as did Charles and Louise Buck's dry cleaning business. It is believed the last to occupy the building was Faith Baptist Church, which closed around 1982. An empty lot now occupies the site (Courtesy of the late Richard Miller.)

Edward Poole helped win the pennant for the Pittsburgh Pirates in the early 1900s, along with the Eastern League in the mid-1900s. It is well documented he played alongside greats such as Honus Wagner, Jimmy Burke, Steve Brodie, Iron Man McGinnity, and Casey. Shown in this photograph in the second row are Poole (second from the left) and Wagner (fifth from the left). (Courtesy of the late Richard Miller.)

MARVIN JENKINS
Vice-president

Not only can Malvern lay a claim to fame with Edward Poole, but also with Marvin Lee Jenkins. A singer, pianist, composer, and songwriter, Jenkins worked alongside legends such as Della Reese, Oscar Brown Jr., and Marvin Gaye. Known for his soul, jazz, and rhythm and blues, he was talented with nearly every type of musical instrument. Jenkins graduated from Malvern High School with the class of 1950.

The current home of the Malvern Historical Society, this building is located at 108 East Porter Street. When this photograph was taken (in July 1908), Hermann and Weaver Meat Market occupied the first floor, while the newspaper *Clay City Times* was printed on the second. Pictured are, from left to right, (first row, seated) Joseph Dewell, Earl Robertson, and Joseph Hermann; (second row, standing) John Weaver, Arthur Wadsworth, Arthur Lewis (news editor), and Augustus Hermann.

William Arthur Lewis was well ahead of his time. Owning multiple businesses, including several groceries and a restaurant, Lewis established the *Clay City Times*, a local paper, in 1908. He was a promoter of the Malvern community band, a talented poet, and a mathematical genius and served as village assessor and mayor. Lewis was also the founder of the *Malvern News*, where he ran historical photographs of Malvern in the 1930s.

In December 1919, W.A. Lewis established the Bee Hive Store after purchasing and combining two other groceries in town. This new store was located in the building that once stood where the parking lot is for the current post office at 116 East Porter Street. Lewis purchased this delivery vehicle around that time, with added stand-out advertising for his business venture.

The Sugar Bowl restaurant is pictured here around 1911. Shown in the photograph are, from left to right, Ben Burwell, Walter Weigand, Joseph Hermann, and Herman Rennier. Rennier was the first casualty of World War I from Malvern. W.A. Lewis operated this restaurant, located at 119 East Porter Street. The brick building housed many businesses, including the post office, bowling alleys, and Malvern Sundries.

Tomlinson's Restaurant, operated by Edward and Nettie Tomlinson, is shown in this 1911 photograph. Pictured are, from left to right, Lee Tomlinson, unidentified, Minnie Tomlinson, Howard "Toots" Tomlinson, and Edward Tomlinson; Nettie Tomlinson is behind the bar. At the time this photograph was taken, the business was located at 117 South Reed Avenue. This building would later house Al Cinson's ABC Barbershop for years.

Little is known about the history of the Malvern depot. The railroad came through Malvern around 1853–1854. Records do not indicate when this building was constructed; however, Jesse Brothers is listed as railroad station agent in 1860. The Cleveland & Pittsburgh Railroad traveled the tracks that brought people to and from Malvern. This building was located at the end of South Reed Avenue, near Robinson Clay Products Plant No. 7.

The Philip L. Thomas Garage Company was located on the southwest corner of the intersection of North Reed Avenue and Canal Street. The former Lewton House stood on this site, which was razed around 1919–1920 to build the brick garage that stands today. Thomas, who is shown second from the left, operated his business here until 1935. The structure was built by Martin Rennie, Dean Rennie, and Ernie Martin.

Laubacher's Service Station was owned by Clarence Laubacher and situated on the east side of his home located at 829 East Porter Street. This photograph was taken in October 1934 and shows Laubacher next to the gas pumps, which dispensed Texaco products. He served the community as fire chief beginning in 1952 and held that position for more than 30 years. (Courtesy of Kay Laubacher Bosh.)

Spratt's IGA store was built in 1939 by R.T. Spratt and was located at 103 West Main Street. He moved his business from next door (west side), which had been located in an aging frame building no longer standing. The Spratt home can be seen at the right; it no longer stands. Other groceries followed here, including Krause's IGA and Robbins's IGA. The building was remodeled and converted into two apartments.

Hermann and Weaver Meat Market was located at 108 East Porter Street; the Malvern Historical Society currently occupies the building. Augustus A. Hermann, who is pictured here around 1924, was operating his business as early as 1908, retired around 1934, and was a business partner with John D. Weaver. This building later became the first location for Woods Grocery, along with serving the community as a library.

HOFFEE HEMMING BLOCK MALVERN, O.

Built in 1903 of Malvern-made bricks, this structure at 100 East Porter Street was initially known as the Hoffee and Hemming Clothing Store, followed by Rice's Clothing. The corner entrance gained access to the Malvern bank, with the second floor once containing the dentist office of Dr. T.C. VanPelt and a telephone switchboard office. The third floor was known as Hoffee-Hemming Hall, which hosted graduations, square dances, and basketball games.

Co-owner Florents E. Hoffee is shown with merchandise at the Hoffee and Hemming Clothing Store at 100 East Porter Street. Entry to the area shown was on the East Porter Street side of the building. The 104 South Reed Avenue entrance led to boots and shoes. The birthplace of Theodore Vail had been moved from this location to make way for this three-story brick building to be constructed in 1903.

Pictured here is a building, formerly at 121 South Reed Avenue, during its demolition in January 1988. An empty lot remains. Built originally as a storeroom, Samuel and Susan Beach resided here in 1920 with many recalling seeing the Civil War veteran seated in a rocking chair in front of one of the large windows. In 1973, Vic Bell opened Malvern Electronics here, servicing radios, televisions, stereos, and tape players.

Cyril A. Ebner, Malvern mayor from 1942 to 1946, opened Ebner's Grocery at 111 North Reed Avenue on April 1, 1921. Pictured here inside the store in this c. 1930 photograph are, from left to right, Leo Lovy, Ebner, Nick Lovy, Louise Buck, and James Lovy. A single gas pump was located at the corner of the sidewalk outside of this building at one time. (Courtesy of the Malvern Historical Society.)

This section of North Reed Avenue has changed considerably with only one of the buildings pictured still standing. An early village hall is pictured at the left. Next in line is Deckman's Furniture Store, which operates today as Crowl Interiors and Furniture. The third building was embellished with the name Kirk at the top and razed in 1996. The former William Burwell residence is at the far right.

Stephen Deckman took his father-in-law into partnership with the furniture and undertaking business in 1900. The business was known as Deckman and Swisshelm from that time until 1915. Pictured here in a wagon advertising the trades of furniture and undertaking are Lee Dell Scott Klotz (left), who was employed at the furniture establishment, and Joseph Swisshelm (right), father-in-law and business partner of Deckman.

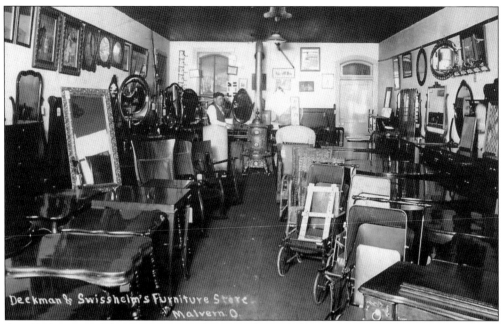

A c. 1908 image of the interior of Deckman and Swisshelm Furniture Store is shown here with proprietor Stephen G. Deckman in the background. The core of this original brick building is still within the walls of Crowl Interiors and Furniture at 403 North Reed Avenue. The structure has had multiple significant changes through the years, with George Deckman founding the furniture business in 1861.

Former Malvern mayor Harry R. Kibler owned this station from 1931 until 1936, which was located at 532 East Porter Street. St. Francis Xavier Catholic Church is pictured in the background. It is unclear when this filling station was removed from the property; however, Curtis Taylor purchased the station and adjoining garage in 1936. Louis Furey established Furey Motor Service here in 1942. (Courtesy of Kay Laubacher Bosh.)

Hollywood Brands owned this building on North Reed Avenue, by the bridge, with operations associated with milk products and candy bars from the 1930s until 1965. The structure was built around 1916 as the Odessa Theater and briefly served as a meeting place for the American Legion. Before this building was constructed, a blacksmith shop occupied the site. This photograph was taken in 1959. (Courtesy of the Malvern Historical Society.)

Daniel A. "Tony" Mason operated Mason's Grocery at 103 North Reed Avenue for decades. He is shown in this 1959 photograph donning his white apron, and many remember him as nearly always having a stubby cigar. During Mason's occupancy, the second floor was the tailor shop of Clarence Swisshelm. The small entryway to the right hosted a number of restaurants/businesses through the years. (Courtesy of the Malvern Historical Society.)

The year 1940 brought about significant changes at 107 North Reed Avenue. The tin and stove shop of William Clark Lewis was razed to make way for Red's Nite Club. This photograph presents a view of what would have been the rear of the building. Lewis operated his business here beginning in 1873 and continued to manage the storeroom for more than 60 years. (Courtesy of Dr. Tom Romano.)

Philip "Red" Romano is posing in front of Red's Nite Club in this 1959 photograph. A native of Italy, Romano constructed this building at 107 North Reed Avenue in 1940, and it remained a hub of activity for downtown Malvern for years. Bowling alleys, air-conditioning, and Coney dogs brought repeat customers regularly. (Courtesy of the Malvern Historical Society.)

Veatrice Thompson is shown giving his grandson Darren Hunt a trim in 1965. Thompson arrived here in 1940 from Alabama for work opportunities. He became the preferred barber for the African American community of Malvern and surrounding areas and opened his residence to neighbors and friends. The Thompson family resided in a small home that was behind a residence currently standing at 109 North Reed Avenue. (Courtesy of Joe Thompson.)

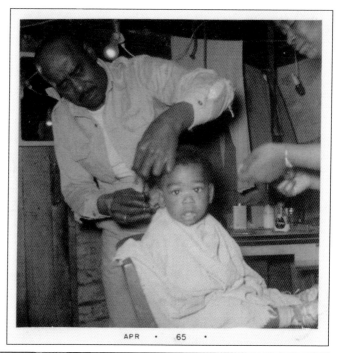

Woods Grocery remained a part of the Malvern scene for many years, with the business being established by Robert Woods in 1953 and later passed to son James. The building pictured here at 111 North Reed Avenue served as the grocery's storeroom beginning in 1959. In 1984, the business moved to the newly constructed headquarters at 5077 Alliance Road NW, where it remained until closing in 2021.

-: HOTEL :-
MALVERN
Reed Ave.   Malvern, O.

Board by the day or week
Regular Meals Served.
Transient business attended
to.   Clean comfortable
rooms.   Auto Service.

"A home away from home"
FRED MARRIOTT
Proprietor.

═══ The ═══
Sugar Bowl
Restaurant

A full line of Candies,
Cigars and Tobacco.
Sanitary Ice Cream by
the pint, quart or gal.

FRED MARRIOTT
Proprietor

Fred Marriott operated both the hotel and a restaurant around 1915–1918. The Sugar Bowl Restaurant was located in a brick building now razed at 119 East Porter Street. The hotel stands at 108 South Reed Avenue and had its own dining room at the time. During lunchtime, Marriott would have an employee leave the restaurant, serve guests in the hotel, and then finish their day back at the restaurant.

This business block at 119 East Porter Street is only a memory now. The dark building housed multiple restaurants, the post office, and later bowling alleys opened in 1948 belonging to Charles and Mary Petrucci. Perry Goff's printing shop was upstairs around World War I. The building at the right was constructed in 1888 as the Commercial Hotel. The Malvern Grill called this side home, as did the Brickyard Lounge.

The Y Tank and Tummy Station was located in the approximate area of 7391 Canton Road NW (near the Y intersection) around 1932. Owned by Herbert and Myrtle Muffly, the filling station and lunchroom also had small cabins where travelers could stay the night. The business was short-lived and changed hands through the mid-1930s. Myrtle is shown third from the left in this photograph. (Courtesy of Cheryl Muffly Czech.)

This early-1920s photograph shows a newly remodeled Oliver's Restaurant and Cozy Corner dining room located at 103 South Reed Avenue. Nelson R. "Doc" Oliver opened it around 1919 and operated his eatery for years, adding the brick front to the original frame building. The structure to the left has advertising on the second-floor windows for the dentist office of Dr. T.C. VanPelt. (Courtesy of the Malvern Historical Society.)

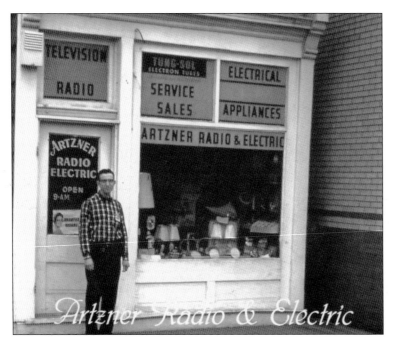

Joseph Artzner is pictured outside of Artzner's Radio and Electric when located at 115 North Reed Avenue in this 1959 photograph. This building still stands. His passion for all things electric developed at an early age. Artzner started displaying and selling radios in Hart's Drug Store at the age of 12. After more than 50 years of serving the community, he retired in 1979. (Courtesy of the Malvern Historical Society.)

Located at the southeast corner of the intersection of North Reed Avenue and Canal Street, Campbell's Sohio station was an institution of its own. Established by John L. Campbell in 1926, his son Wayne would eventually take over the business. The building pictured was razed in December 1998. (Courtesy of the Malvern Historical Society.)

John and Rhoda (Buck) Krider operated a store in a building that once stood between 105 and 117 West Main Street. An empty lot remains. Krider purchased this two-story building in 1897 and is shown here, at the left, around 1899. R.T. Spratt would also operate his IGA store in this spot before building his new neighboring storeroom in 1939. (Courtesy of Larry and Norma Taylor.)

Employees at the Taylor Chevrolet and Oldsmobile garage are shown among period automobiles at 532 East Porter Street. Curtis Taylor purchased this business in 1936 from Harry Kibler, who also dealt with the Chevrolet brand. Pictured are, from left to right, Taylor, Robert Downs, Oscar Lewis, Clarence Laubacher, unidentified, and Louis Furey. Furey later purchased the business and opened Furey Motor Service. (Courtesy of Kay Laubacher Bosh.)

ABC Barber Shop - Albert Cinson

ABC Barbershop was located at 117 South Reed Avenue with owner Albert B. Cinson, pictured here in 1959. The business opened at this location in 1944 following his return home from serving with the US Navy during World War II. A local hot spot for gathering and camaraderie, the doors closed in October 1992. Cinson was known for providing a free first haircut for children. (Courtesy of the Malvern Historical Society.)

Proprietor Louis Romano is shown in this 1959 photograph outside of Romano's Home and Auto Supply Store. A son of Italian immigrants and part of a large family, Romano served the community at this location, which was across from the former drive-in movie theater, for many years. This building still stands at 4029 Coral Road NW. (Courtesy of the Malvern Historical Society.)

Works Progress Administration (WPA) employees are pictured in this 1930s photograph. This work-relief program was one of many during the Great Depression, which, through this crisis, provided women a stronger workforce presence. Sewing, school programs, and recreational work were some of the jobs that may have been secured by those pictured, who remain unidentified. (Courtesy of the Malvern Historical Society.)

Evelyn Foltz is pictured at the Kopper Kettle restaurant in this photograph taken by Elton Pretty in 1959. This building, on East Porter Street, no longer stands. The Malvern Historical Society is currently in the building to the left. Take note of the pay phone booth sandwiched between the buildings. This restaurant would change locations, moving a few buildings west to the corner of the square. (Courtesy of the Malvern Historical Society.)

One of Malvern's favorite summertime hangouts is the Dairy Queen located at 310 West Canal Street. This photograph dates to 1959 and shows Margie Romano (left) and Kate Angeloni (right) in front of their business. Traffic from the next-door Malvern Village Park helps keep business steady at this location. (Courtesy of the Malvern Historical Society.)

From 1969 until 2000, the Malvern Branch Library touched many lives throughout its time spent at 108 East Porter Street. This photograph dates to 1993. In 2000, a new brick library was constructed, and this location was vacated, with the Margaret Woods family graciously donating this historic building to the Malvern Historical Society. The building continues to serve the community as a museum for this nonprofit organization.

Six

HOMETOWN BEAUTY

Looking out over Malvern in this c. 1910 photograph reveals a thriving village at the peak of its clay product industry. The grounds of Robinson Clay Products Plant No. 7 are clearly visible, with multiple smokestacks and kilns along with the depot, which can be seen at mid-left. The roadway heading into the distance on the right is Bridge Street, with the cupola of St. Martin Lutheran Church visible.

This stereoscopic view card appears to date to around 1890 and shows a primitive scene with wooden sidewalks and sapling trees. The home at the far left is standing at 217 East Porter Street. The storefront shown is marked as "Wilson's Store" and was roughly where 223 East Porter currently stands. The next two homes remain at 229 and 231 East Porter Street. (Courtesy of the Malvern Historical Society.)

An early view looking toward the square, likely in the early 1890s, shows a home still standing on the left at 110 North Reed Avenue. The next small building was the drugstore of James G. Murdock. Following in line was a two-story building that housed George Wingerter's Barbershop for years. In the distance, on the right, is the birthplace of Theodore Vail, located at 100 East Porter Street.

The cameraman was standing roughly at the intersection of Canal and Canton Streets, near the rear of present-day Crowl Interiors and Furniture, when this photograph was taken. From left to right are the rear of the former Malvern Village Hall, the Malvern Mills, the Sandy and Beaver Canal, a small frame building that later became part of Campbell's Sohio station, and the Lewton House hotel.

"Wall Street" was a nickname given to this section of North Reed Avenue in the 1850s. This early-1890s photograph shows, from left to right, Deckman's Furniture Store, L. Boerner's bakery and confectionery, B. Cunningham's Cigars, Charles G. Deuble's jewelry and silverware, the Bee Hive Store, and at far right was a home once located at 101 West Main Street. (Courtesy of Kathy Bortz.)

An exceptionally rare outdoor scene of Oneida taken around 1860 depicts a thriving community. The house at the right still stands as the restored Patrick C. Hull home at 8187 Blade Road NW. The large multistory building next to it was the Oneida Mill. A planing mill appears to be directly across from the home, with the former two-story post office building partially hidden behind it.

The large Oneida Mill is shown at the left in this c. 1908 photograph. The street separating the mill from the other buildings is present-day Blade Road NW, with the railroad tracks visible to the extreme right. The two-story frame building in the center was James Harsh's store and also served as the Oneida Post Office. All buildings pictured are no longer standing.

One building remains out of this early-1900s scene. Pictured is the Dr. William R. and Nancy (Thompson) Spratt home standing at 117 West Main Street. Partially visible at the left is Spratt seated in front of his doctor's office. The home at the right was an early structure no longer standing and judging by architectural details was likely built in the early 1840s. (Courtesy of Kelly Nypaver.)

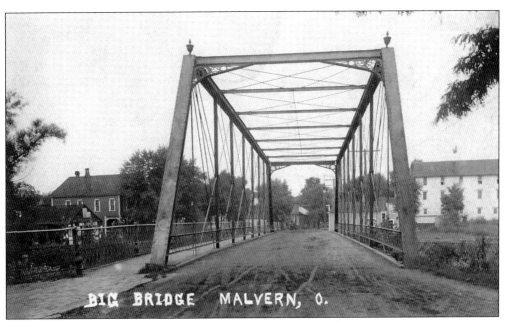

Today's bridge, which spans Sandy Creek on North Reed Avenue, barely compares to its monstrous predecessor. Buildings shown in the photograph include a blacksmith shop, which is visible through the guardrail at the left; the George Deckman home; and the towering mill at far right. The cameraman would have been standing at Water Street looking north when this was taken in 1910.

Built in 1878, this cast-iron bridge was deemed unsafe by residents around the late 1930s. However, during demolition, some news articles stated the bridge was so sturdy it refused to be knocked down and had to be dismantled by hand. Razed in 1940, at least one other known bridge was on this site prior to 1878.

A period automobile travels alone on North Reed Avenue heading north toward the 1878 bridge. This photograph dates from the 1920s. The building at the right still stands at 203 North Reed Avenue and housed a hardware store for many years. Malvern streets were brick-paved at this time in history, which fared well with gas-powered vehicles becoming commonplace. (Courtesy of Kay Laubacher Bosh.)

William McMillen is shown with Malvern's water wagon on the bridge in this c. 1910 photograph. Prior to 1915, all streets in town were dirt, and during dry weather, this created dusty conditions. With the use of this horse-powered vehicle, these conditions were kept under control. The wagon had its own place to fill up at a pipe protruding near the falls at the mill's forebay.

This is possibly the only known photograph in existence of a wooden footbridge that spanned the old Sandy and Beaver Canal at Plain Street. The present-day lumberyard is behind those standing on the bridge, with some West Main Street homes (still standing) in the background. The bridge was a common shortcut for schoolchildren who resided on the south side of the village.

It is believed this aerial shot of Malvern dates from the 1940s. Reed Avenue is pictured winding through town with the three-story Malvern Mills visible near the center. Robinson Clay Products Plant No. 7 is shown in the distance at center. The state route had not come through at the time of this photograph, which maintained the peaceful setting of the village.

Taken in 1909, this photograph shows the old cast iron bridge at Oneida and the railroad depot. The photographer would have been standing on Blade Road NW looking toward present-day Alliance Road NW. Philip Summers and Willard Crowl were past station agents. No date of construction has been found for this building; however, it does appear on a map dating to 1874.

Bethlehem Cemetery has confirmed burials back to 1822 with some unmarked graves likely predating this. The mausoleum of Dr. Enoch C. Ross and family is shown here in this c. 1910 photograph and still stands, being constructed of Malvern-made bricks. Bethlehem Presbyterian Church originally stood in this cemetery prior to moving to the final East Porter Street location.

The Hardesty cemetery contains remains of some of Malvern's founders, including 36 known burials dating from 1836 through 1883. The cemetery (or adjoining ground) is said to contain the graves of two escaping slaves. Abolitionist Rev. William Hardesty aided them along the route of the Underground Railroad, and lore has it, they perished while in his care, and he laid them to rest on his property.

The water tower, or standpipe as some called it, stood atop a hill near East Main Street overlooking the village for decades. This hill was nicknamed "Standpipe Hill" by many, with Malvern receiving a waterworks system in 1912. Rev. Gerald Carl lettered the Malvern name as shown in the photograph in 1987. In 1999, the tower was demolished, forever changing the skyline that so many had grown accustomed to. (Courtesy of Lee Faa.)

Perched next to the former water tower was another iconic symbol of Malvern. A 69-foot flag pole, constructed by Malvernites, was installed with the help of a helicopter and paid for by community donations in November 1971. Travelers could see Old Glory from some distance arriving into town. In 1999, the pole was removed, and a new display was created at the Malvern Village Park.

Originally built during World War II days, this wall of honor contained the names of men and women fighting for freedom at that time. Originally constructed facing East Porter Street and situated near where the current post office parking lot meets the building, the display disappeared many years ago. The structure at the left housed the state liquor store for years.

Robbins Street is named in honor of Lee R. Robbins, one of the original founders of the First Baptist Church of Malvern. He was responsible for having the cluster of homes built around this church to provide housing for others of the African American community arriving at Malvern to work in the clay industry. Robbins was also the owner of a grocery store that operated out of his home for decades.

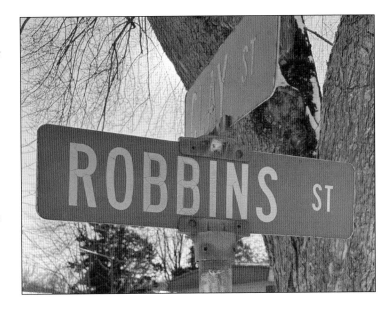

The public square consists of the intersection of Porter Street and Reed Avenue. This photograph dates to around 1910 and looks east on Porter Street. The three-story Hoffee-Hemming building at the right was constructed in 1903 and advanced downtown dramatically. Streets remained dirt until 1915. The building at the left housed the barbershop of George Wingerter for many years. A carriage stepping stone is shown in the left-bottom corner.

Standing at 108 South Reed Avenue is an imposing structure built as a hotel, possibly in the 1880s. Name changes over time have included Wagner House in 1891, Jones House in 1899, Hotel Park in 1909, and Hotel Malvern around 1918. Charles Stadelman also owned the hotel in the 1910s. Frank Fleming opened a barbershop in the basement in 1891, and many years later, Charles Romano opened up a poolroom.

This unique perspective looking into Oneida dates to around 1910. The photographer would be standing on present-day Blade Road NW looking into Oneida. The mammoth mill is seen at the left and at one time was operated by Ulysses G. Thompson. The milling industry helped to make many small communities in the area prosper.

Residents gather in awe over the power of Sandy Creek as it swells and overruns its banks. Taken Labor Day 1913, this scene shows the bridge to the right and a view looking onward following North Reed Avenue. Flooding was a common occurrence, with this image showing water making its way clear to Main Street.

Through development, the area pictured here has changed drastically. Pictured are, from left to right, Lela Hoffee, Ella D. Ross, and Mabel Hoffee. The trio are in a garden owned by the Hoffee family beside their North Reed Avenue home. A bank drive-through currently occupies this garden spot. Across the street at center is a building still standing at 118 North Reed Avenue and occupied by Waneda's Diner.

West Main Street looks quite barren in this early-1900s photograph. The photographer would have been standing where Avondale Avenue is presently. At the time of the photograph, that street had not been created yet. At left is the 1891 schoolhouse, and next to it is a home standing at 503 West Main Street. All the homes on the right are still standing.

Dirt streets were still the norm when this photograph was taken around 1908. This view is captured on West Porter Street, near the intersection of Canton Street. The home on the left still stands at 117 West Porter Street. Malvern's first telephone office was located in the small building to the right, with one of the first operators being Viva Dumbleton.

An early-1895 view of West Main Street, near the intersection of Canton Street, was developed from a glass plate negative. Looking east toward North Reed Avenue, the large building at the right was the Deckman Furniture Factory. On the opposite side of the flat-roofed building is the present-day Malvern Village Hall at 116 West Main Street, with the remainder of the buildings beyond that still standing.

The east side of the Malvern Mill is shown in this photograph, with the waters of the forebay within view. The mill changed hands many times through the years until it was demolished in 1959 for the completion of State Routes 183/43. The final business to occupy the building was the Malvern Feed and Supply, owned by Clyde Blanchard.

This is another early view of downtown Malvern looking toward the square. Buildings are barely visible due to the number of trees lining the streets. The current Victoria Building, which houses the Contini Insurance Agency, is shown at the left with the old hotel next to it. The tall building at the right burned in 2009 and housed Pizza Works/Pizza Rack during its final years.

REED AVENUE
MALVERN, OHIO

Judging by the curbs installed along this section of South Reed Avenue, it helps to date this picture to at least 1915. All the homes at the right still stand and at that time were occupied by (from near to far) Laubender, Jupenlatz, Lewton, Fisher, and Crissinger. This area of town was extremely busy, as the depot would have been near the photographer, along with Robinson Clay Products Plant No. 7.

The snowstorm of 1950 buried Malvern, as shown in this scene on South Reed Avenue. The buildings were occupied by, from left to right, ABC Barbershop, Buck's Dry Cleaning, and the Malvern Variety Store. The center building, once belonging to early baseball player Edward Poole, has been razed, while the other two are still standing.

Around 1900, downtown had an elevated bandstand attached to the side of a building that once stood at 103 North Reed Avenue. Band members were required to climb a ladder to reach the lofty stage, all while lugging their instruments. Live music was offered every Saturday night and on special occasions. This must have been a short-lived idea, as the bandstand disappears from photographs early on.

The Malvern Citizens Band proudly poses outside of a home still standing at 103 East Main Street sometime in the 1890s. Pictured are, from left to right, two unidentified, Stephen Deckman, William Arthur Lewis, three unidentified, John Fisher, unidentified, Henry Vinton Buel, Harry Haskey, and unidentified. Of note is Buel, who was a veteran of the Spanish-American War.

Jumping up a number of decades, Lake Mohawk is a private, man-made lake of 507 acres and was established in 1963 by the American Realty Service Corporation. This photograph dates to September 1963 and shows some early development. In 1965, offshore lots were being sold for $1,295. (Courtesy of Kay Laubacher Bosh.)

The Y, which allows travelers to either head toward Minerva or Carrollton, changed with the addition of State Routes 183/43. This photograph from 1959 shows a building no longer in existence, which was owned by Robertson's Plumbing and Heating. The building at the extreme right still stands and houses Crossroads Pizza at 7400 Canton Road NW. (Courtesy of the Malvern Historical Society.)

West Main Street is lined with picket fences in this c. 1905 photograph. Looking east, the home at the right still stands on the west side of the lumberyard. This home was built by Frederick Buel, likely in the early 1870s. Buel, along with his brother-in-law Joseph Fishel, established the Fishel and Buel Lumber Company, which remains a dealer in lumber products under the name of Crowl Lumber Company.

Once again, the tree-lined streets nearly make the homes vanish from the scene in this c. 1910 photograph. The photographer would have been standing on the north side of East Porter Street, near the former First Christian Church (currently Linwood Apartments), and looking west. Streets are still dirt in this image, but sidewalks appear to have been advanced to brick.

Porter Street - East

Morning sunlight is illuminating downtown Malvern in this 1959 photograph, complete with a traffic light. This image takes the reader to a time when buildings lined the streets and businesses filled their rooms. To the right is a sign for Hart Drugs, with a drinking fountain out front. Today, the opposite side of East Porter Street has lost all the buildings pictured. (Courtesy of the Malvern Historical Society.)

Some may say it is just a bridge, but to think of the cars that have driven, feet that have walked, parades that have marched, and funerals that have processed, it takes on a different meaning. The North Reed Avenue bridge pictured was built in 1940 and replaced in 2006. (Courtesy of Lee Faa.)

Wagon wheel tracks mark the lanes on West Main Street in this 1908 photograph. The home at the left still stands, with the current Malvern Village Hall next in line at 116 West Main Street. Across the road are horse-hitching posts in front of John D. Krider's store, which no longer stands. In 1885, Krider set up shop to become a broom maker, which he continued for a number of years.

A unique vantage point is seen in this photograph of the south side of Deckman's Furniture Store. The old Sandy and Beaver Canal bed is in the foreground next to a small frame building that served as Malvern Village Hall prior to 1915. Records state a bank was in this small building in 1858, which deemed this block the nickname "Wall Street." (Courtesy of the Malvern Historical Society.)

This corner of West Main Street and North Reed Avenue has been a hub of activity since the beginning of the village. The sign hanging from this building advertises Herman Nice's home furnishings, dishes, and novelties. It is difficult to envision Erma Vandegrift's thriving restaurant here and the amount of foot traffic this building has seen. In the background is the former John D. Krider grocery, followed by R.T. Spratt grocery.

Oliver's Restaurant and Confectionery opened shop here around 1919 at 103 South Reed Avenue. In the 1940s, this corner was a pickup and drop-off point for the Blue Ridge bus lines route. The original part of the building is of frame construction and is back from the sidewalk a number of feet. Oliver added the brick front, bringing his business level with the others. (Courtesy of Kay Laubacher Bosh.)

Being on one of the main streets, this home at 116 North Reed Avenue has witnessed a lot of downtown happenings. The residence was built by Joseph Fishel, who was co-owner of the lumberyard. Pictured here in 1907 at Merle Brown's birthday party are, from left to right, (first row) Bertha Reed, Esther Maurer, Mable Stackhouse, and Helen Ruff; (second row) Vivian Hemming, Harold Smith, Brown, ? Caldwell, and Paul Reed.

A busy downtown scene on the square is represented in this 1940s photograph. The crowd gathered near Joseph Artzner's public address, sound, and amplification vehicle, with much of this equipment built and designed by the owner. His motto was "Our business is sound." In the background is Hart Drugs. The building to the left is the current home of the Malvern Historical Society.

Some great details are present in this c. 1910 photograph, including the buggies, row of hitching posts, and the antiquated water fountain on the north sidewalk. The arched doorway at the right on this brick building led to the upper floors. A sign is displayed here with a bell on it that alerts the public the phone office is in the corner room on the second floor.

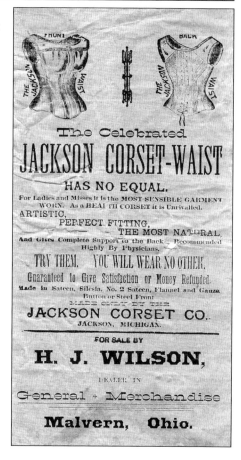

One of the few artifacts left to represent the business of H.J. Wilson is this envelope advertising the sale of corsets. Wilson owned a general store, and it moved to multiple locations within town. The building attached to this envelope's history was located on East Porter Street across from the current Malvern Historical Society. The entire block of buildings has been razed.

Oneida Mills, as it was called in the 19th century, supported a hefty milling business. This building was constructed to receive its power from the Sandy and Beaver Canal, with evidence still remaining of the canal's pathway. This c. 1908 photograph reveals, at the extreme bottom-right corner, part of the decorative fence from the Patrick C. Hull and later Ebenezer Hudson McCall home at 8187 Blade Road NW.

This is a panoramic bird's-eye view of Oneida around 1908 as taken by area photographer I.T. Brothers. This taker of images seemed to explode with business around this year. Shown in the image at mid-right is the Oneida Mill from the backside of the community. The cluster of homes at the left would be on Old Canal Lane NW today.

A sad scene presents with this photograph of the Malvern depot dated 1940. Only a ghostly shadow outlining where the Malvern sign had once been displayed remains. Records do not indicate when the building was shuttered. Situated at the end of South Reed Avenue, the amount of visitors this building saw throughout its existence would be staggering to fathom.

Having a vehicle was a big deal when this photograph was taken. This c. 1912 image shows three Malvern men out for a drive. Pictured are, from left to right, Herman Rennier, who was the first casualty from Malvern during World War I; Daniel A. "Tony" Mason, who operated a grocery on the square for decades; and Frank Black, one-time head superintendent of all Robinson Clay Products plants in Ohio.

Malvern has always been a fan of parades, as evidenced by this early-1900s photograph. A patriotic theme pervades advertising the Malvern Clay Company as being the pioneer of Sandy Valley. Pictured are, from left to right, unidentified, William Worley, and Stephen Deckman. The Malvern Clay Company changed names in 1908, which helps to date the image.

Overlooking the village from the southwest perspective, this 1908 photograph depicts a growing community. Robinson Clay Products Plant No. 7 is shown at the right with its many smokestacks, while the tracks of the Cleveland & Pittsburgh Railroad seem to bisect the image. West Grant Street, from South Reed Avenue going west, was just in its planning phase.

Campbell's Sohio station occupied the southeast corner of the intersection of North Reed Avenue and Canal Street for a number of years. The bridge is shown at the extreme right, and just beyond that is the former Corner Café (currently the Firehouse Grill) at 122 North Reed Avenue. (Courtesy of Michael Campbell.)

Winters were different in 1950. Cooper and Elsie Rice are standing in front of Rice's Clothing Store on the square looking east down Porter Street. The sign for Hart Drugs is next in line, followed by the grocery of Cline and Scurto. In the distance on the opposite side of the street is the former Malvern Grill.

Many bargains were had at the Malvern Flea Market when located in the Victoria Building on the square. Ken Hutchison is pictured waving to the photographer. The right side of the building sported a pay phone, and the water fountain was still on the East Porter Street side of the building. (Courtesy of Lisa Palczewski.)

Generations have called the Malvern and Oneida areas home. The people have made the communities what they are today, with descendants of some of the earliest pioneers remaining. Pictured here in 1896 are Carl Thompson (left) and his brother Fred Thompson (right), both from a well-founded family. (Courtesy of Florence Thompson Untch.)

BIBLIOGRAPHY

Albacete, M.J. *Clyde Singer's America*. Kent, OH: the Kent State University Press in cooperation with the Canton Museum of Art, 2008.

Albrecht, Ralph L. *A Commemorative History of the Malvern Area Centennial*. Carrollton, OH: Carrollton Standard Printing Company, 1969.

Beers, J.H. *Commemorative Biographical Record of the Counties of Harrison and Carroll, Ohio*. Chicago, IL: J.H. Beers and Company, 1891.

Eckley, H.J., and William T. Perry. *History of Carroll and Harrison Counties, Ohio*. Chicago and New York: The Lewis Publishing Company, 1921.

Gard, R. Max, and William H. Vodrey. *The Sandy and Beaver Canal*. East Liverpool, OH: East Liverpool Historical Society, 1952.

Green and White Malvern High School Annual, 1950.

Hardesty, H.H. *Illustrated Historical Atlas of Carroll County, Ohio*. Chicago, IL: H.H. Hardesty, 1874.

Lewis, W.A. "Malvern is Pioneer Clay City of United States." *Canton Daily News* (June 3, 1928): 8.

McCollam, C. Harold. *The Brick and Tile Industry in Stark County, 1809–1976*. Canton, OH: Stark County Historical Society, 1976.

DISCOVER THOUSANDS OF LOCAL HISTORY BOOKS
FEATURING MILLIONS OF VINTAGE IMAGES

Arcadia Publishing, the leading local history publisher in the United States, is committed to making history accessible and meaningful through publishing books that celebrate and preserve the heritage of America's people and places.

Find more books like this at
www.arcadiapublishing.com

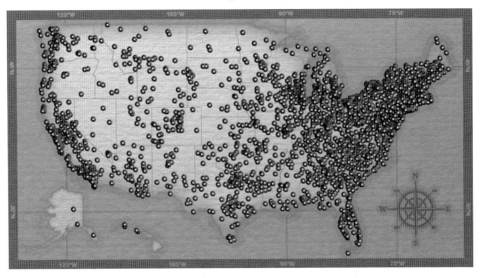

Search for your hometown history, your old stomping grounds, and even your favorite sports team.